BRAIN GA

'50s
Remember
When?
PICTURE PUZZLES

pil

Publications International, Ltd.

Contributing writer: Holli Fort

Cover puzzle photo: Phil Toy

Back cover puzzle photos: Shutterstock.com

Interior puzzle photos: Getty: 6, 32, 41, 42, 43, 46, 114; Library of Congress, Prints & Photographs Division, LC-DIG-ppmsca-06616: 113; Library of Congress, Prints & Photographs Division, LC-USZ62-135184: 64; Library of Congress, Prints & Photographs Division, NYWT&S Collection: 34, 35, 47, 48, 61, 78, 87, 90, 98, 99, 112, 116, 120, 126, 128, 138; Library of Congress, Prints & Photographs Division, Toni Frissell Collection: 86; Library of Congress, Prints & Photographs Division, U.S. News & World Report Magazine Collection: 14, 28, 29, 76, 77, 80, 82, 84, 110, 111, 123; Media Bakery: 10, 109; Movie Stills DB: 49, 105, 124; NASA: 118, 119; PIL: 12, 24; Shutterstock.com: 7, 8, 9, 11, 15, 16, 17, 18, 20, 22, 23, 25, 26, 30, 31, 36, 37, 38, 40, 44, 50, 51, 52, 54, 55, 56, 57, 58, 60, 62, 63, 65, 66, 68, 69, 70, 71, 72, 74, 75, 79, 83, 85, 88, 91, 92, 93, 94, 96, 97, 100, 102, 103, 104, 106, 108, 117, 122, 125, 129, 130, 131, 132, 134, 135, 136, 137, 140; Phil Toy: 19

Louis Weber, CEO
Publications International, Ltd.
7373 North Cicero Avenue
Lincolnwood, Illinois 60712

Permission is never granted for commercial purposes.

ISBN: 978-1-68022-034-6

Manufactured in China.

8 7 6 5 4 3 2 1

Put Your Eagle Eyes to the Test ▪ 4

Level 1 ▪ 6

Start off with easy puzzles that feature nostalgic photos with just a few changes.

Level 2 ▪ 41

Pick up the pace and hone your observational powers with these vintage photos.

Level 3 ▪ 76

Search these retro scenes carefully as the changes increase and become more subtle.

Level 4 ▪ 109

Travel back in time as you test your mettle against these more challenging puzzles.

Answers ▪ 141

Put Your Eagle Eyes to the Test

Are you ready to put your eagle eyes to the test? The puzzles in this book will be sure to test your powers of observation. Just look carefully at the photos on each page and try to spot the differences between them. But be warned—the puzzles get more difficult in each level! The number of changes increases and the differences will be harder to spot.

In this book, the familiar Picture Puzzle format is given a special 1950s spin. You'll browse through vintage photos from the period, be reminded of events that happened and objects that were invented during the decade, and even learn some fun '50s trivia.

As you move through the book, you'll sharpen your observational skills. Pay close attention, because the changes may be found in the smallest details. Not all puzzles feature just two images. Some puzzles involve finding a single change hidden among a group of multiple copies of the same image. You'll need to look carefully at all the photos to determine which one is not like all the others. If you're stumped, you can always get a hint from or check your work against the answer key located at the back of the book. The original picture is presented in black and white, with the changes circled and numbered.

Challenging your brain and focusing your attention are fun ways to keep your mind fit and relaxed during your busy days. And with our '50s theme, you'll have the pleasure of nostalgia, too! So get ready, clear your mind, and get started!

A Trip Down Memory Lane

1. Which toy debuted in the 1950s?

    A. Barbie   B. G.I. Joe   C. Slinky

For more about '50s toys, see page 37.

2. Which territory became a U.S. state in January 1959?

    A. Arizona   B. Alaska   C. Hawaii

For more information on the territories that achieved statehood in the 1950s, see pages 54–57.

3. Poodle skirts were generally made of this material.

    A. Cotton   B. Felt   C. Polyester

For more about '50s fashion, see page 43.

4. This company began using "TV dinner" in its marketing in the '50s.

    A. Swanson   B. Tyson   C. Green Giant

For more about the development of the TV dinner, see page 10.

5. The remote control debuted in December 1959.

    True   False

For more about the remote control, see page 58.

1. A. 2. B. 3. B. 4. A. 5. False

Mid-Century Mix-Up

Furniture took an intriguing turn in the 1950s with the introduction of mid-century modern styles. Chairs, tables, and other furniture ranged in style from severe architectural fashions to more kitschy looks, like the chair seen here. New technologies allowed for the production of the more organic looks favored during this period.

Answers on page 141.

Dream Car Challenge

Pedal cars—miniature versions for kids—started out as toys for wealthy children, but they were widely available by the 1950s. Many of the toy cars had features just like the full-size models, including working lights, ragtops, whitewall tires, and hood ornaments. Today, an original 1955 Chevrolet pedal car would fetch about $1,750.

Rice, Rice Baby

Have a happy occasion finding all the changes.

Answers on page 141.

Care to Wiffle?

Fun '50s fact: Wiffle ball was first played in 1953.

1

2

3

4

5

6

Answer on page 141.

Defrosted Dinner

There is some debate as to who actually invented the TV dinner, but this freezer mainstay enjoyed an explosion in popularity starting in 1954, when Swanson began to manufacture the convenience food. Whether Swanson invented the frozen meal or not, it was definitely the first company to use the phrase *TV dinner* in its marketing.

Answers on page 141.

TV Tray Treat

We're serving up a full helping of changes in this TV dinner!

Jailhouse Jumble

Here's some Elvis trivia for you! His prison haircut in *Jailhouse Rock* (1957) was long a source of speculation among fans: Was his infamous ducktail actually cut? The truth is that wigs were used to represent the short haircut and the haircut when it was partially grown back. Plaster casts were made of Elvis's head to fit the wigs precisely and make them nearly impossible to detect.

©Metro-Goldwyn-Mayer (MGM)

5 changes

Meet You at the Station

Looking for changes is just the ticket at this 1958 picture of Union Station, Washington, D.C.

Answers on page 142.

Shore Span

Fun '50s fact: Michigan's Mackinac Bridge, one of the longest suspension bridges in the world, was built in the 1950s.

All Keyed Up
A sharp eye is the key to finding the single change.

1

4

2

5

3

6

Answer on page 142.

Currency Carrier

Can you find all the changes in this piece of '50s currency? We think you've got it in the bank.

Blue Plate Special

We're open 24 hours for you to spot the changes!

Answers on page 142.

Cruisin' Along

Enjoy the view of this 1957 Chevrolet Corvette while you find the changes.

Marquee Event

Geometric shapes, the use of glass and neon, and a futuristic look characterized the "Googie" architecture trend that was popular in the 1950s.

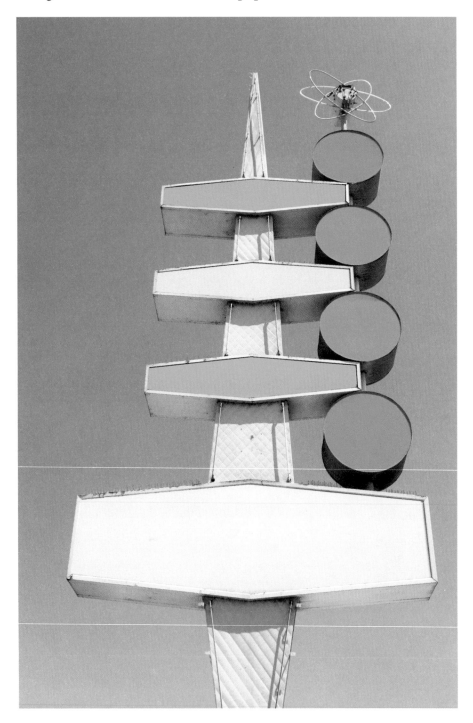

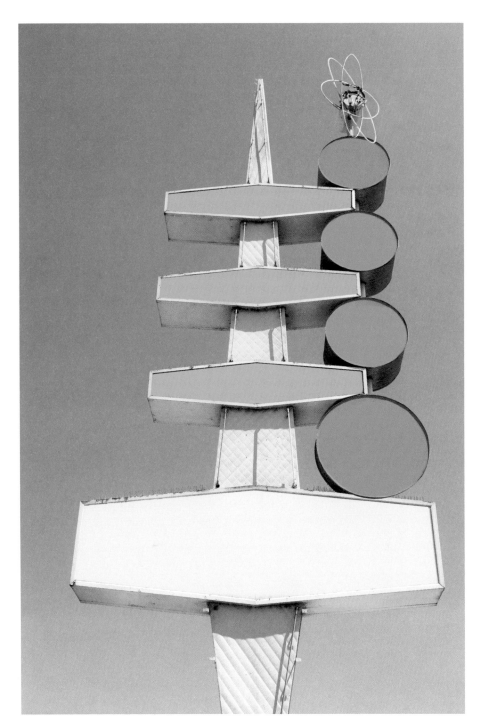

Reel-to-Reel Changes

In 1948, Ampex developed the first reel-to-reel tape machines for commercial use. The new technology was snapped up by networks and radio personalities who recognized the value of pre-recording their programs for later broadcast. Reel-to-reel tape machines stayed popular until the advent of the cassette recorder in the 1960s.

Answers on page 143.

Table for Two

Dinette tables with Formica tops and stylized chrome legs were a hallmark of 1950s dining style. Formica, a high-pressure laminate, was so popular that by the early 1950s, a third of new homes in America used it. Laminates made by Ohio-based Formica Company truly were ubiquitous in 1950s Americana.

Crosstown Classic

The bitter rivalry between the Brooklyn Dodgers and New York Yankees was well established by the 1950s. Between 1949 and 1956, the teams faced each other in the World Series five times, with the Yankees usually emerging victorious. In 1955, the Dodgers managed to defeat the Yanks in seven games, but by 1956 (shown here), the Yankees were back on top.

Answers on page 143.

Lunch Box Locator

Vintage lunch boxes like these are among the most collectible memorabilia of the 1950s and beyond. Some popular lunch boxes, such as the Hopalong Cassidy and Roy Rogers models, now range in value from hundreds to thousands of dollars.

1

4

2

5

3

6

Soda Fountain Search

Pull up a stool in this classic eatery as you search for changes.

Cable Guy

This 1958 picture shows a man working a movie projector in a theater. Popular movies in that year included *The Blob, Cat on a Hot Tin Roof*, and *Vertigo*.

Answers on page 144.

Crib Course

There's no kidding around if you want to find all the changes at this child's nursery.

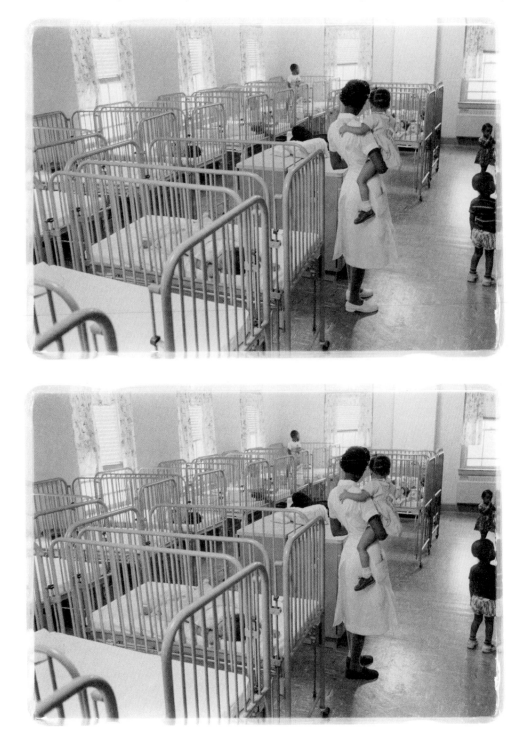

A Clean Sweep

You just need to find the single change and you'll be all cleaned up!

1

4

2

5

3

6

Answer on page 144.

Behind the Wheel

Don't dash around—be deliberate in finding all the changes in this car's dashboard.

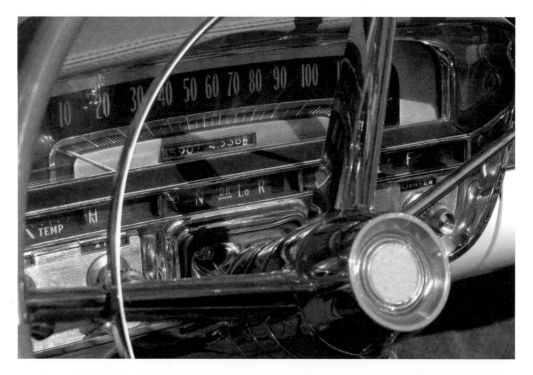

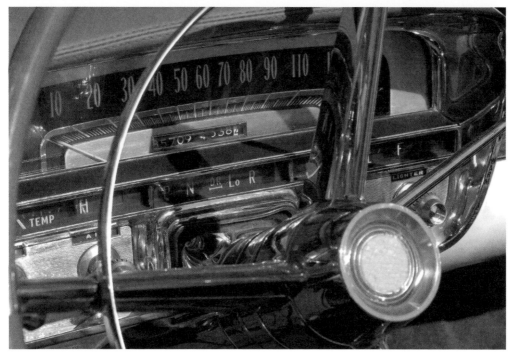

Cinema Classic

The beloved musical comedy *Singin' in the Rain* premiered in 1952. If you like the famous dance sequence where Gene Kelly twirls an umbrella, you might be even more impressed to know that Kelly filmed the scene while ill with a high fever.

Bit of a Stretch

Give your mind a workout by searching for all the changes in this 1956 picture.

Answers on page 145.

Piano Men

This 1952 picture shows musician Benny Goodman (third from the left) in rehearsal with his group. Popular for decades, Goodman was known as the "King of Swing."

Leaf Well Enough Alone

Fun '50s fact: We're not blowing hot air when we say that the leaf blower was another invention of the 1950s.

Set Phasers to Stun

Rayguns were one popular kid's toy during the 1950s. Some other toys that hit the market in the 1950s included Mr. Potato Head (1952), Play-Doh (the mid-1950s), and Barbie (1959).

1

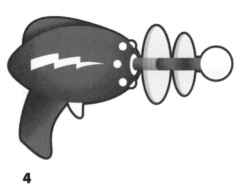

4

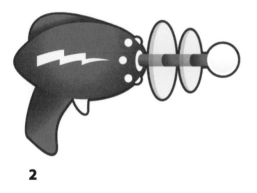

2

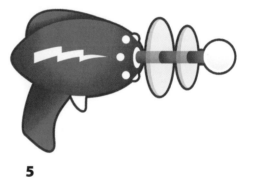

5

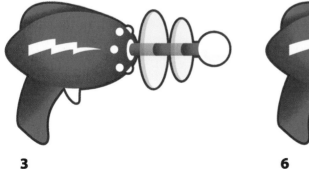

3

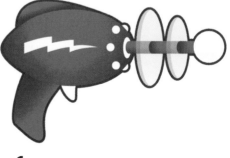

6

Propped Up

Let your eyes fly around this picture of an aviator from the mid-1950s.

A Sign of Things to Come

Can you point to all the changes?

Answers on page 145.

Lollipop, Lollipop

In the postwar era, car sales were up, and the family road trip was the preferred vacation for many Americans. The interstate highway system was developed during the 1950s, leading people to travel faster and farther than ever before—on a good day, a car of the era could travel 350 miles! The country's national parks were extremely popular family destinations.

Retro Radio

By the end of World War II, 95 percent of homes had radios, but the emergence of television in the early 1950s led most radio stations to reduce news and dramatic segments while increasing the amount of music played. And as rock 'n' roll gained popularity, it filled many of the holes left in radio programming schedules and helped radio retain its relevancy.

Answers on page 146.

It's a Date

If only one piece of clothing could exemplify 1950s fashion for young women, it would be the poodle skirt. This full skirt was generally made of bright felt, with a poodle appliquéd to the lower section and a leash (often sparkly) winding up toward the waist. A sweater or blouse, scarf, ponytail, bobby socks, and saddle shoes most often completed the ensemble.

Kitschy Kitchen

By the late 1950s, American middle-class prosperity led to bold design and color choices, particularly in kitchens. In 1954, General Electric began producing appliances in different color choices, and the competition immediately took notice. Soon, American consumers had their choice of a veritable rainbow of decorating options.

Go . . . Fight . . . Win!

Can you tackle the differences between these '50s football photos? Find them all, and you'll be a champion!

Answers on page 146.

Sidewalk Sale

Browse through this 1955 picture of New York's Garment District and rack up the differences.

Sweet Soxers

Put your best foot forward and find the single change!

1

4

2

5

3

6

Answer on page 147.

Dramatic Debut

Fun '50s fact: The 1956 movie *Love Me Tender* was Elvis's debut movie.

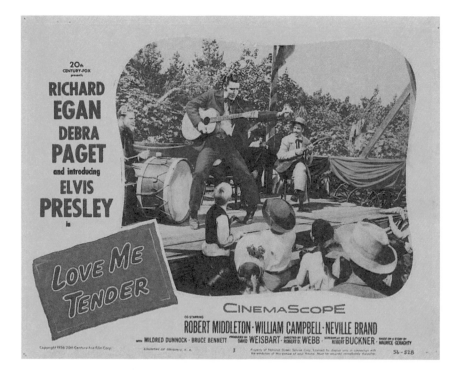

Peak Performance

Fun '50s fact: On May 29, 1953, Edmund Hillary and Tenzing Norgay reached the summit of Mt. Everest. Theirs was the first confirmed ascent of Earth's highest mountain.

Answers on page 147.

Out to Lunch?

Find the stack of changes hidden in this picture!

Squeeze Box Stroll

We're in accord…it's time to find some changes!

Welcome to Alaska

Fun '50s fact: Alaska became the 49th state on January 3, 1959.

Juneau the Way

Alaska is the largest U.S. state by area.

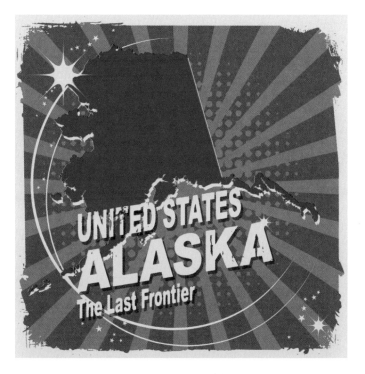

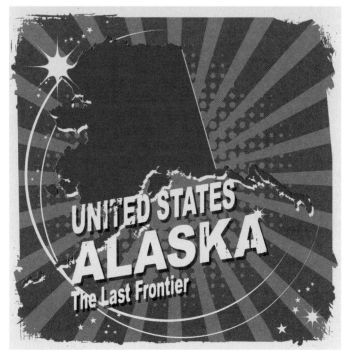

Swift and Shore

Fun '50s fact: Hawaii became the 50th state on August 21, 1959.

Answers on page 148.

Postcard Perfect

Hawaiian-themed luaus were very popular in the 1950s.

1

4

2

5

3

6

Beam Me Up

Fun '50s fact: The first television remote control, produced by Zenith, hit the market in 1950.

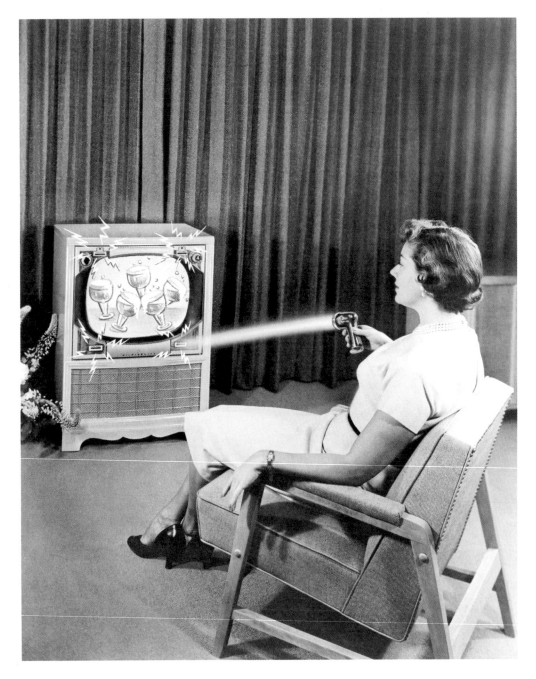

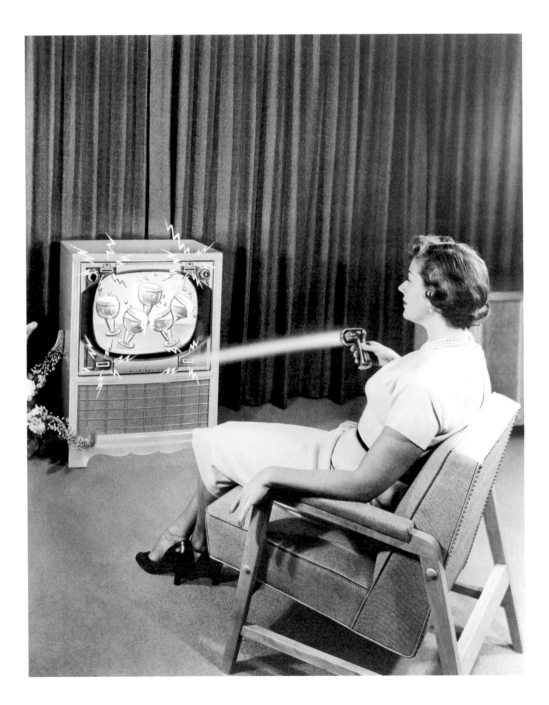

Antique Auto

Both exterior and interior modifications were very popular in the 1950s, and car customizers would often display their finished products at drive-in restaurants to help drum up business, a practice that continues today.

Answers on page 148.

Corner the Market

To market we go, to find all the changes in the 1956 photo....

Entertainment Central

Time to face the music and find the changes.

Traipsing Trio

Find the single change in this fabulous '50s family photo!

1

4

2

5

3

6

An Open Concept

This photo houses some challenging changes.

Seat Yourself

Get to work in finding the changes in this group of colleagues.

Top of the World

It might look simple, but the changes add up.

An Arch Look

These 1953 tourists admire Paris's Place du Carrousel. Can you spot the changes?

Answers on page 149.

A Leg Up?

Fun '50s fact: Pink flamingo lawn ornaments date back to the 1950s, when they were wildly popular.

Keeping Tabs

Fun '50s fact: This everyday invention, the bread clip, dates back to 1952.

Answers on page 150.

Neon Night

Take a gamble on finding the single change.

1

4

2

5

3

6

Answers on page 150.

Up in Your Grille

You're on the road to finding the differences....

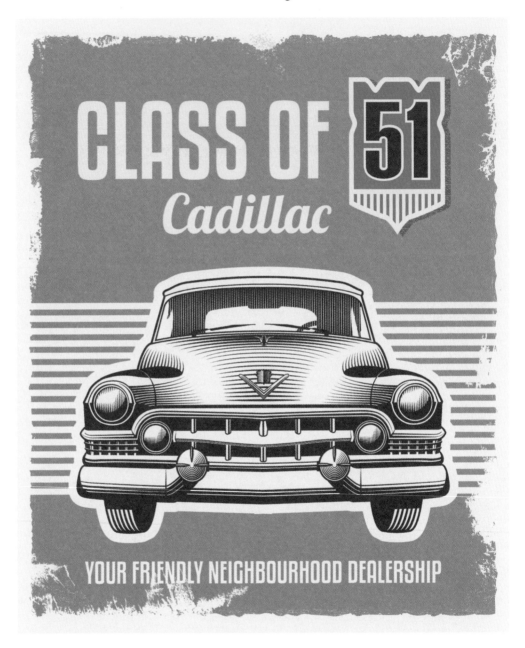

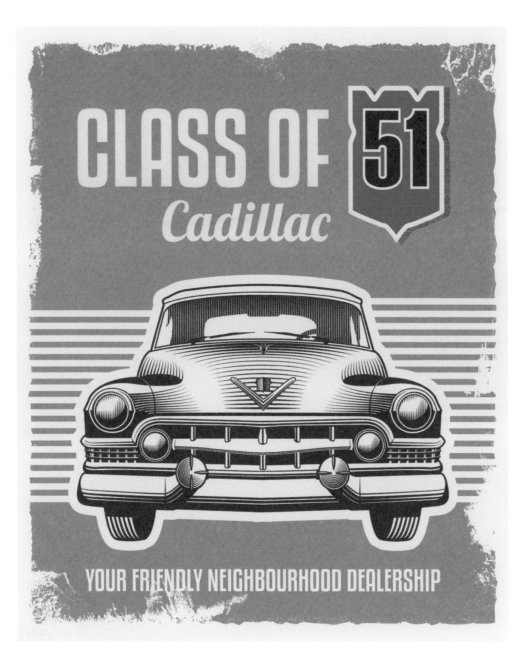

The Static Quo

Tune in and you'll be sure to spot the changes.

Answers on page 150.

Immobile Home

The post-World War II housing shortage led to a rise in the number of trailer parks like this one.

Face the Nation

Here, President Eisenhower gives a speech about science and national security. The white object is the nose cone of an experimental missile that had gone into space.

Answers on page 151.

Presidential Parlez

This 1955 photo shows President Dwight D. Eisenhower at the White House with Lyndon B. Johnson, who served as a Senator from 1949 to 1961.

In the Mists of Time

Don't let the smog obscure the single change.

1

4

2

5

3

6

Answer on page 151.

Diner Delights

In 1950, the average American spent 32 cents on every dollar on food. That kind of investment could buy plenty of burgers, milkshakes, and French fries at the local diner! But people didn't just flock to diners for the food—diners were considered prime locations for teenagers to go on dates or to casually hang out together.

Answers on page 151.

Evening Ritual

We've introduced a few changes to this picture of cozy family life.

A Fare Fight

You're about to go on a journey to find the changes.

Answers on page 151.

Quantum Mechanics?

You're guaranteed to find some changes in this picture.

Hot off the Press

Stop the presses! It's time to spot the changes in this 1957 newsroom.

Accessories After the Fact

Find the single change in this vintage evening set.

1

2

4

5

3

6

Pier into the Past

We've served up some changes to this 1957 photo of a family going to play tennis.

Answers on page 152.

The Corner Office

Shine a light on the changes in this 1952 photo.

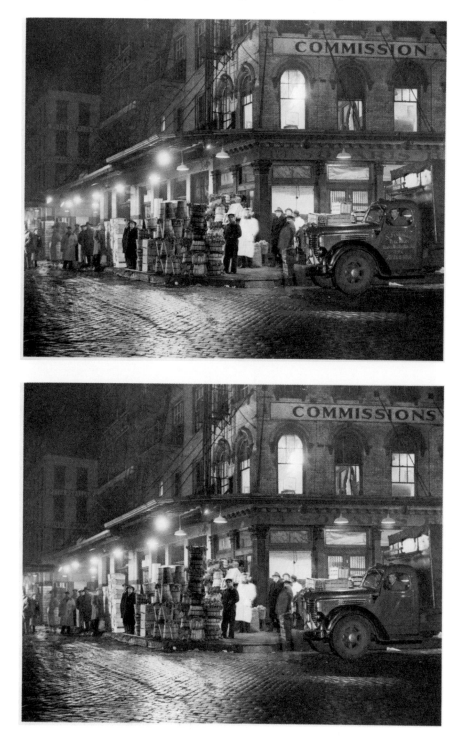

Yolk It Up

Looks like a recipe for change....

Permission to Board

Pull up to the dock to find the differences.

Answers on page 153.

Gravy Train

Are you on board with finding the changes?

Under the Counter
Take a seat and spot the changes.

At the Drive-Thru

National Parks such as Sequoia National Park were one popular destination for family vacations in the 1950s.

1

4

2

5

3

6

A Game of Hoops

Fun '50s fact: Modern hula hoops were invented in 1958.

Wedding Bell Bliss

Take steps to find the changes in this '50s wedding photo.

Answers on page 153.

Command Center

Some of these changes just don't compute....

A Fresh Start

This produce market has produced a fine crop of changes!

Answers on page 154.

In a Jam
Don't delay on finding the changes in this 1951 photo.

Postwar Boom

This picture shows Levittown, one of the first and most influential suburbs that sprang up in the United States after the war.

State Dinner Setting

Time to meet and go over the changes.

Signs of the Times

Fun '50s fact: America's first yield sign debuted in Oklahoma in 1950.

Boxed In
Don't toy around—jump in and find the single change!

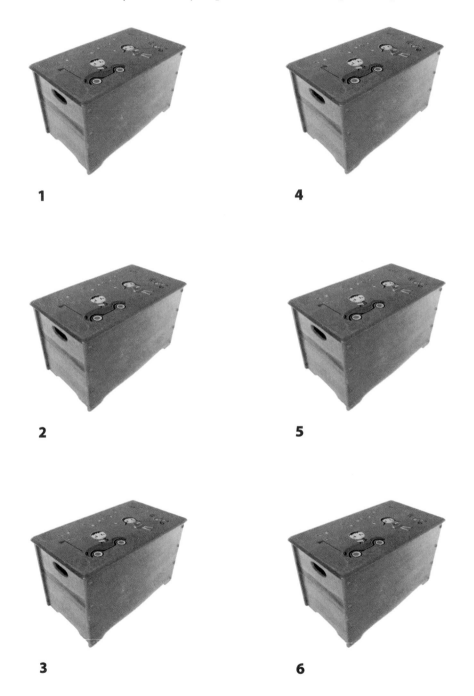

1

4

2

5

3

6

Answer on page 155.

On the Silver Screen

The Thing from Another World, one of many science-fiction movies that opened in the 1950s, was released in 1951. Other popular sci-fi movies from the '50s included *Destination Moon*, *The Day the Earth Stood Still*, *Creature from the Black Lagoon*, and *Attack of the 50 Foot Woman*.

Answers on page 155.

A Tall Order

Roller skating was a popular pastime in the 1950s, and carhops sometimes used roller skates at drive-through restaurants.

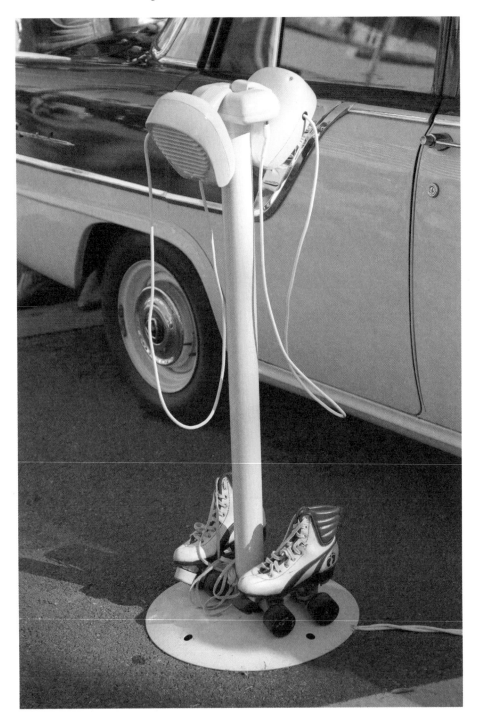

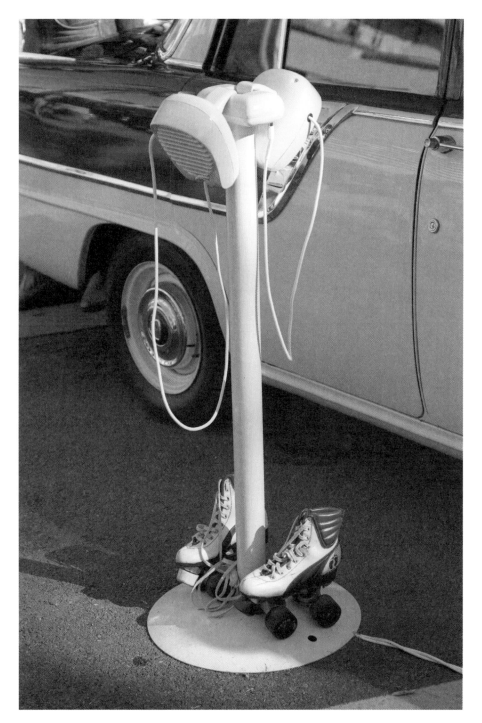

Sunday Drivers
Visit sunny Miami for a dollop of changes.

Answers on page 155.

TV Time

In the '50s, TV rapidly gained popularity in the United States—but there wasn't always something to watch. Most national network shows were broadcast in the afternoons and evenings. And at some times of the day, all you saw was static!

Made in the Shade

The backyard barbeque was a 1950s suburban tradition. Are you fired up to find the changes?

Answers on page 155.

Old School

Find the changes before the school bell rings!

Sorry Sight

Famous catcher Roy Campanella played for the Brooklyn Dodgers from 1948–1957. It's your turn to catch the single change in this picture!

1

4

2

5

3

6

Answer on page 156.

Game On!

Go on, take a swing at finding all the changes.

Icebox Inquiry

Like many innovations of the time, refrigerators began to be mass-produced after World War II, and by the 1950s, most households were putting them to good use. One notable exception (at least on television) was the Kramden household of *Honeymooners* fame—they had an old-fashioned icebox, which symbolized Ralph and Alice's financially strapped status.

Here's the Deal

Let's go shopping for some changes!

Answers on page 156.

By the Numbers

Fun '50s fact: The first paint-by-numbers kit cropped up on the market in the 1950s.

1 change

Run Aground

Fun '50s fact: NASA was formed in 1958. The aircraft in this 1954 photograph were owned by NASA's predecessor, NACA (National Advisory Committee for Aeronautics).

1

4

2

5

3

6

Answer on page 157.

Hangars On

You'll need a keen eye to spot the changes in these NACA aircraft.

A Coney Island Treasure

Stop off for a full serving of changes!

Diner Bell

A true diner is a restaurant in the shape of a railroad dining car because some of the first diners were fashioned from old train cars or trolleys. The heyday of the diner took place in the 1950s, when they were not only a place to get a freshly prepared meal, they were also social gathering places and popular hangouts for teens.

Answers on page 157.

Smooth Operators

These switchboard operators needed to be sharp—and so do you, to spot the changes!

Positively Hitchcockian

James Stewart and Grace Kelly starred in the well-reviewed Alfred Hitchcock thriller *Rear Window* (1954). Can you spot all the changes in this publicity still?

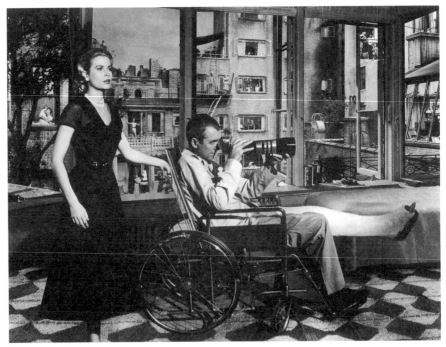

© *Paramount Pictures. Answers on page 157.*

Fenced In

Look all around the neighborhood for the single change.

1

4

2

5

3

6

Answer on page 158.

Beacon Call

This lighthouse shows the way to some changes.

Balancing Act

You'll find a bushel of changes in this 1954 photo.

Answers on page 158.

Wheeling and Dealing

Rev up to find all the changes in this period poster!

Keeping Time

Practice makes perfect, when it comes to playing music or finding changes.

Answers on page 158.

Suit Yourself

Dive in and find the single change!

1

2

3

4

5

6

Full Stop

Fun '50s fact: Before 1954, stop signs used black text against a yellow background. The 1954 redesign introduced the red-and-white coloring scheme we're familiar with today.

Out-Classed

Time for a class photo—and for a search for changes.

Answers on page 159.

The Best Thing on Two Wheels

Toot your own horn if you can find all the changes!

1 change

A Cut Above

Are you tempted to find the single change?

1

2

3

4

5

6

Answer on page 159.

Hold That Note

Get on board with finding the changes!

Catching Some Rays

This alien visitor (based on the 1951 movie *The Man From Planet X*) has brought changes that are out of this world!

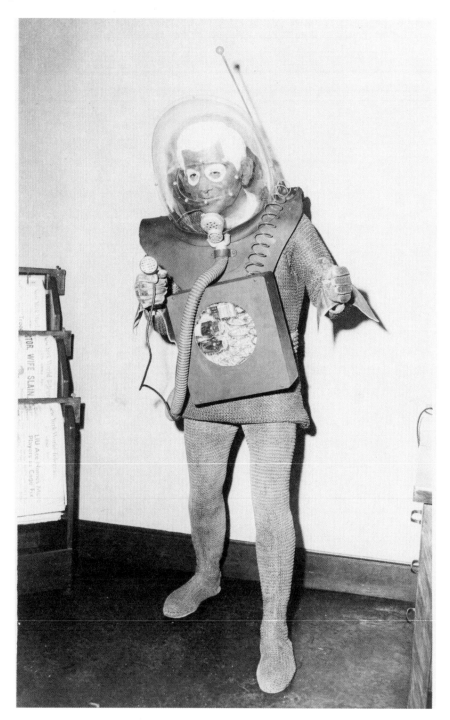

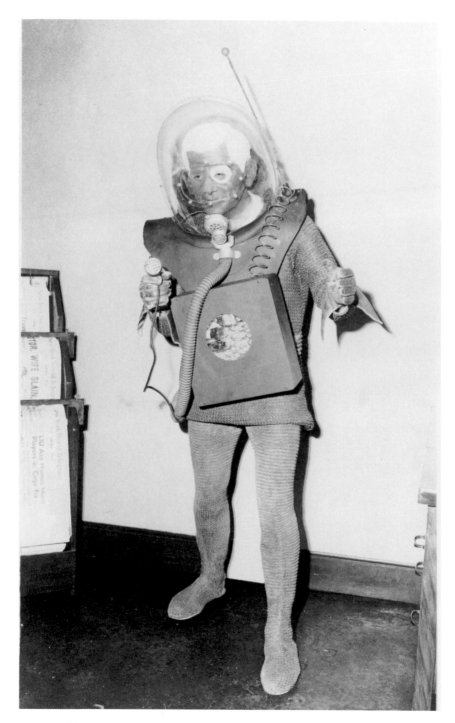

Answers on page 159.

Double Feature

The number of drive-in theaters skyrocketed in the 1950s. By 1958, there were close to 5,000.

Answers on page 160.

LEVEL 1

■**Mid-Century Mix-Up** *(page 6)*

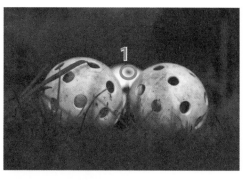

■**Care to Whiffle?** *(page 9)*
Picture 5

■**Dream Car Challenge** *(page 7)*

■**Defrosted Dinner** *(page 10)*

■**Rice, Rice Baby** *(page 8)*

■**TV Tray Treat** *(page 11)*

Jailhouse Jumble (pages 12–13)

All Keyed Up (page 16)
Picture 2

Meet You at the Station (page 14)

Currency Carrier (page 17)

Shore Span (page 15)

Blue Plate Special (page 18)

■**Cruisin' Along** *(page 19)*

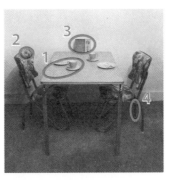

■**Table for Two** *(page 23)*

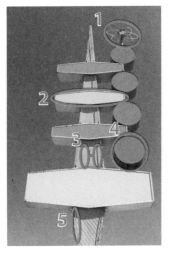

■**Marquee Event** *(pages 20–21)*

■**Crosstown Classic** *(page 24)*

■**Lunch Box Locator** *(page 25)*
Picture 3

■**Reel-to-Reel Changes** *(page 22)*

Soda Fountain Search (pages 26–27)

A Clean Sweep (page 30)
Picture 1

Cable Guy (page 28)

Behind the Wheel (page 31)

Crib Course (page 29)

Cinema Classic (pages 32–33)

■**Bit of a Stretch** (page 34)

■**Set Phasers to Stun** (page 37)
Picture 4

■**Piano Men** (page 35)

■**Propped Up** (pages 38–39)

■**Leaf Well Enough Alone** (page 36)

■**A Sign of Things to Come** (page 40)

LEVEL 2

■Lollipop, Lollipop *(page 41)*

■Kitschy Kitchen *(pages 44–45)*

■Retro Radio *(page 42)*

■Go...Fight...Win! *(page 46)*

■It's a Date *(page 43)*

■Sidewalk Sale *(page 47)*

■**Sweet Soxers** *(page 48)*
Picture 6

■**Out to Lunch?** *(page 51)*

■**Dramatic Debut** *(page 49)*

■**Squeeze Box Stroll** *(pages 52–53)*

■**Peak Performance** *(page 50)*

■**Welcome to Alaska** *(page 54)*

Juneau the Way *(page 55)*

Swift and Shore *(page 56)*

Postcard Perfect *(page 57)*
Picture 3

Beam Me Up *(pages 58–59)*

Antique Auto *(page 60)*

Corner the Market *(page 61)*

■**Entertainment Central** *(page 62)*

■**Seat Yourself** *(page 65)*

■**Traipsing Trio** *(page 63)*
Picture 6

■**Top of the World** *(pages 66–67)*

■**An Open Concept** *(page 64)*

■**An Arch Look** *(page 68)*

■**A Leg Up?** *(page 69)*

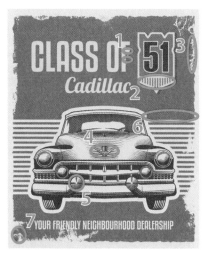

■**Up in Your Grille** *(pages 72–73)*

■**Keeping Tabs** *(page 70)*

■**The Static Quo** *(page 74)*

■**Neon Night** *(page 71)*
Picture 1

■**Immobile Home** *(page 75)*

LEVEL 3

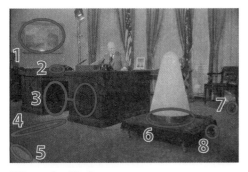

■**Face the Nation** *(page 76)*

■**Diner Delights** *(page 79)*

■**Presidential Parlez** *(page 77)*

■**Evening Ritual** *(pages 80–81)*

■**In the Mists of Time** *(page 78)*
Picture 5

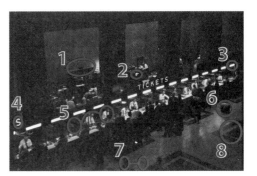

■**A Fare Fight** *(page 82)*

■Quantum Mechanics? *(page 83)*

■Pier into the Past *(page 86)*

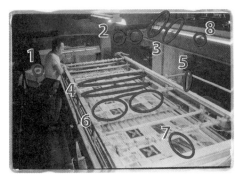

■Hot off the Press *(page 84)*

■The Corner Office *(page 87)*

■Accessories After the Fact *(page 85)*
Picture 6

■Yolk It Up *(pages 88–89)*

Permission to Board (*page 90*)

At the Drive-Thru (*page 93*)
Picture 2

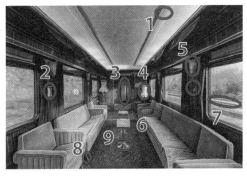

Gravy Train (*page 91*)

Under the Counter (*page 92*)

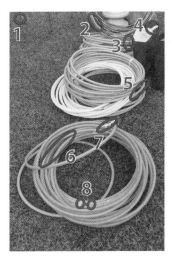

A Game of Hoops (*pages 94–95*)

Wedding Bell Bliss (*page 96*)

■Command Center *(page 97)*

■Postwar Boom *(pages 100–101)*

■A Fresh Start *(page 98)*

■State Dinner Setting *(page 102)*

■In a Jam *(page 99)*

■Signs of the Times *(page 103)*

■Boxed In *(page 104)*
Picture 4

■Sunday Drivers *(page 108)*

■On the Silver Screen *(page 105)*

LEVEL 4

■TV Time *(page 109)*

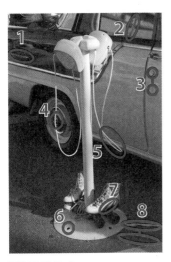

■A Tall Order *(pages 106–107)*

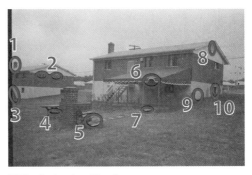

■Made in the Shade *(page 110)*

■Old School (*page 111*)

■Icebox Inquiry (*pages 114–115*)

■Sorry Sight (*page 112*)
Picture 6

■Here's the Deal (*page 116*)

■Game On! (*page 113*)

■By the Numbers (*page 117*)

■Run Aground *(page 118)*
Picture 4

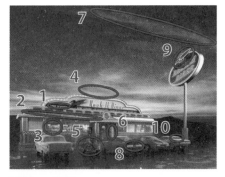

■Diner Bell *(page 122)*

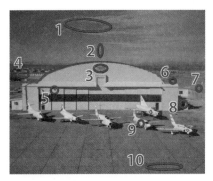

■Hangars On *(page 119)*

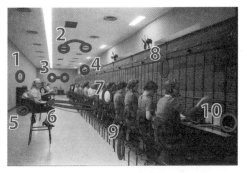

■Smooth Operators *(page 123)*

■A Coney Island Treasure *(pages 120–121)*

■Positively Hitchcockian *(page 124)*

■Fenced In (page 125)
Picture 1

■Wheeling and Dealing (page 129)

■Beacon Call (pages 126–127)

■Keeping Time (page 130)

■Balancing Act (page 128)

■Suit Yourself (page 131)
Picture 2

Full Stop (pages 132–133)

Out-Classed (page 134)

The Best Thing on Two Wheels
(page 135)

A Cut Above (page 136)
Picture 5

Hold That Note (page 137)

Catching Some Rays (pages 138–139)

■**Double Feature** *(page 140)*

Any Bitch Can Party Cookbook
500 Caddy Circle
Pagosa Springs, Co. 81147
970-731-4416   970-731-5516 Fax

Please send_____copies of your cookbook at $19.95 per copy. Please

Add $4.95 for postage and handling. Colorado residents add 8 % sales tax per

cookbook. Enclosed is my check or money order for $_____.

Name:_____

Address:_____

City, State. Zip:_____

Any Bitch Can Party Cookbook
500 Caddy Circle
Pagosa Springs, Co. 81147
970-731-4416   970-731-5516 Fax

Please send_____copies of your cookbook at $19.95 per copy. Please

Add $4.95 for postage and handling. Colorado residents add 8 % sales tax per

cookbook. Enclosed is my check or money order for $_____.

Name:_____

Address:_____

City, State. Zip:_____